Looking at Countries

THE
CONGO

Kathleen Pohl

W
FRANKLIN WATTS
LONDON•SYDNEY

This edition first published in 2008 by Franklin Watts

Franklin Watts
338 Euston Road
London NW1 3BH

Franklin Watts Australia
Level 17/207 Kent Street
Sydney, NSW 2000

First published in 2008 by Gareth Stevens Publishing
1 Reader's Digest Road
Pleasantville
NY 10570-7000 USA

Copyright © Gareth Stevens, Inc. 2008
Series design and concept, and text on pages 30–31 copyright © Franklin Watts 2008

Dewey number: 916.724
ISBN: 978 0 7496 8242 2

Senior Managing Editor: Lisa M. Guidone
Senior Editor: Barbara Bakowski
Creative Director: Lisa Donovan
Designer: Tammy West
Photo Researchers: Sylvia Ohlrich and Charlene Pinckney
Reading consultant: Susan Nations, M.Ed.

Photo credits: (t=top, b=bottom, l=left, r=right)
Cover (main) Schalk Van Zuydam/AP Images; Cover (inset) Per-Anders Pettersson/Getty Images; title page
Martin Harvey, Gallo Images/Corbis; p. 4 Marcus Wilson-Smith/Alamy; p. 6 Cyril Ruoso/JH Editorial/Minden
Pictures; p. 7t Konrad Wothe/Minden Pictures; p. 7b Bruce Davidson/Nature Picture Library; p. 8 De
Agostini/Getty Images; p. 9 Karl Ammann/Corbis (2); p. 10 Schalk Van Zuydam/AP Images; p. 11t Maurizio
Gambarini/Landov; p. 11b Euan Denholm/Reuters/Landov; p. 12 Eddie Gerald/Alamy; p. 13t Rodrique Ngowi/
AP Images; p. 13b Jacques Jangoux/Alamy; p. 14 Eddie Gerald/Alamy; p. 15t Sebastian Bolesch/Das
Fotoarchiv/Peter Arnold; p. 15b Martin Harvey, Gallo Images/Corbis; p. 16 Schalk Van Zuydam/
AP Images; p. 17t Nic Bothma/Corbis; p. 17b Robert Caputo/Aurora Photos; p. 18 Steve Turner/Alamy;
p. 19t Jacques Jangoux/Photo Researchers; p. 19b David Wall/Alamy; p. 20l Gary Cook/Alamy; p. 20r
Emilio Ereza/Alamy; p. 21 Mark Renders/Getty Images; p. 22 Nigel Cattlin/Photo Researchers; p. 23t
Jacky Naegelin/Landov; p. 23b AP Images; p24t Michel Euler/AP Images; p. 24b Howard
Burditt/Reuters/Landov; p. 25 Jose Azel/Aurora Photos; p. 26 Shutterstock; p. 27t Konrad Wothe/Minden
Pictures; p. 27b Per-Anders Pettersson/Getty Images. Every attempt has been made to clear copyright. Should
there be any inadvertent omission please apply to the publisher for rectification.

Printed in China

Franklin Watts is a division of Hachette Children's Books, an Hachette Livre UK company.
www.hachettelivre.co.uk

Contents

Where is the Congo?

The Congo is in Central Africa. Its full name is the Democratic Republic of the Congo. The Congo shares borders with nine other countries. To the west is the Republic of the Congo. Although the two country's names sound similar, these countries are quite separate.

Did you know?

The Democratic Republic of the Congo is the third-largest country on the continent of Africa.

EUROPE

Atlantic Ocean

AFRICA

Indian Ocean

DEMOCRATIC REPUBLIC OF THE CONGO

The Democratic Republic of the Congo makes up much of Central Africa.

Boats carry people and goods along the River Congo.

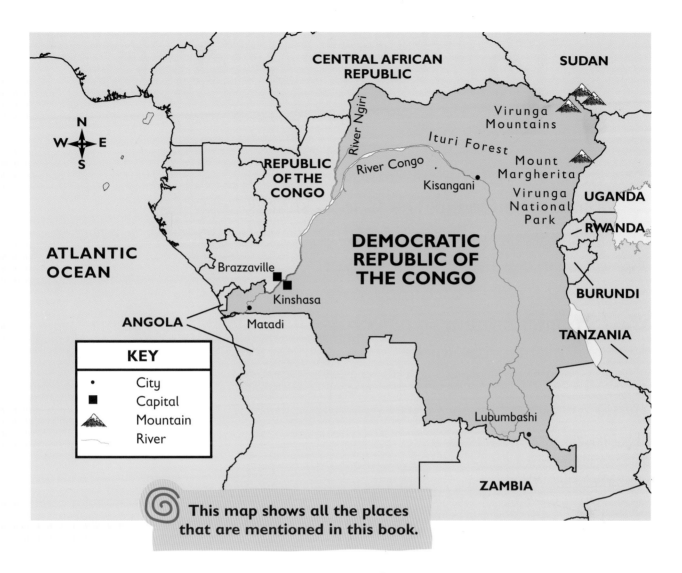

🌀 **This map shows all the places that are mentioned in this book.**

To the north of the Congo are the Central African Republic and Sudan, with Uganda, Rwanda, Burundi and Tanzania to the east. Zambia and Angola lie to the south.

Kinshasa is the capital and the country's biggest city. It has some tall, modern buildings and new homes. It also has some very poor areas with unmade roads.

The River Congo flows through much of the country. It is the fifth-longest river in the world and the second-longest river in Africa.

The landscape

The northern half of the Congo is covered by a huge rainforest, the second-largest in the world. Many tall trees grow there. Their leaves form a roof, called a canopy, over the forest. Thousands of different kinds of plant grow in the rainforest. Some of them do not grow anywhere else. Many animals live in the rainforest.

Did you know?

The bonobo, a type of ape, is one of the closest living relatives of human beings. It lives in the Congolese rainforest.

Bonobos live in a small area of rainforest south of the River Congo.

The Congo has savannas in the south. These are areas of grassland with very few trees.

Mountains rise high in the east. Gorillas and baboons make their home there. Some of the mountains are volcanoes.

The River Congo flows through most of the country. It is an important waterway. People use boats to ship goods and to travel along the river.

This frog adds its call to the sounds of the rainforest.

Mount Nyamulagira, part of the Virunga mountains in eastern Congo, erupted in 2006.

Weather and seasons

The climate in the Congo is tropical. It is very hot and wet most of the year. The hottest area is the rainforest. Thunderstorms are very common.

The savannas are cooler and drier. Sometimes rain does not fall for months. Animals such as lions, buffalo, zebras, giraffes and antelope live there.

A herd of buffalo graze on the dry savanna grasses.

Did you know?

The Congo lies on the equator, the invisible line that encircles the Earth.

Mud keeps this hippo cool in a swamp in the Virunga National Park.

The sun rises and sets at the same time, every day of the year, in the Congo.

In the east, breezes help keep the mountains cool. Temperatures can drop to freezing at night. Snow caps some of the mountains.

Congolese people

More than 60 million people live in the Congo.
Most live near the River Congo or in the highlands.
One in three people is very poor.

Most people in the Congo came from other parts
of Africa long ago. Today, more than 200 ethnic
groups live in the Congo. Sometimes the
groups fight with each other. Fighting
between groups within a country is
called civil war.

Many Congolese women wear bright, colourful clothing. Some wear scarves on their heads.

These people are attending a Roman Catholic church service.

Did you know?

Native people in the Ituri Forest in the north live much as their ancestors did 2,000 years ago.

A native woman rests after collecting firewood in the eastern Congo.

Half of the Congolese people are Roman Catholic, others are Protestant. Some people follow African religions and a few are Muslim.

The official language of the Congo is French. It is spoken in schools and government offices. There are also four national languages and hundreds of local ones.

School and family

Children between the ages of six and twelve must go to school, although many do not. The schools have little money for teachers and books.

More boys than girls go to primary school. All students have to take a test to get into middle school and some go on to high school. Others stay at home and work with their families.

Lunch is served! Half of the children in the Congo go to church-run schools.

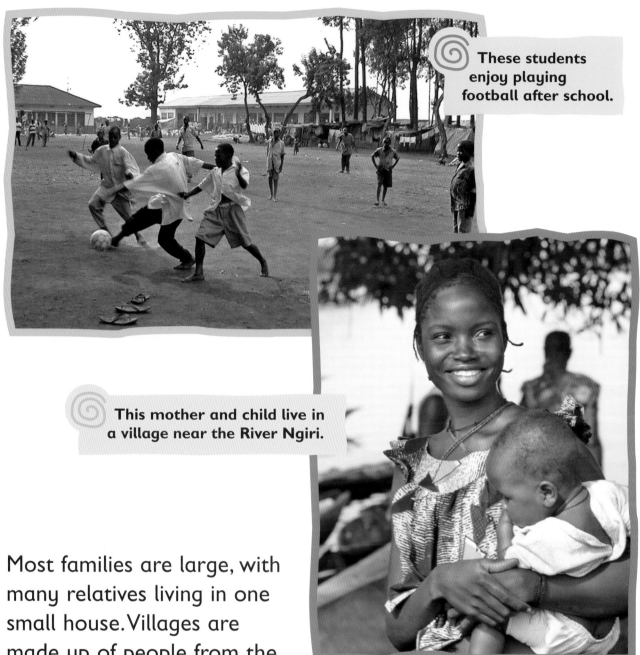

These students enjoy playing football after school.

This mother and child live in a village near the River Ngiri.

Most families are large, with many relatives living in one small house. Villages are made up of people from the same ethnic group.

Women in the Congo do not have the same rights as women in some other countries. Fathers sometimes choose husbands for their daughters.

Did you know?

Half of the people in the Congo are younger than 15 years old.

Country

Seven out of ten people live in the countryside. Most are farmers, struggling to grow enough to feed their families. Many people are very poor.

Farmers grow yams, which are like sweet potatoes. They also grow cassava, a root vegetable, and plantains, which are like bananas. Corn, rice, peanuts and sugar cane are important crops. People raise goats, sheep, cows and pigs.

A woman tends her cabbage plants.

Did you know?

Millions of people in the Congo eat the roots of the cassava plant every day. They eat the leaves as green vegetables.

This woman is carrying water on her head.

These Congolese women have collected firewood for cooking.

Women usually work in the fields. They gather wood and cook over open fires. Most villages do not have electric lights or running water. Fewer than half of the people in the Congo have clean drinking water. They must walk a long way to get water from a river.

City

Some people come to the cities to look for work. Kinshasa, the capital, is home to six million people. It has tall office buildings and art museums, a college and a big sports stadium.

Some people in Kinshasa have good jobs but many are very poor. The rich people live in modern suburbs with clean, paved streets, electricity and street lights.

Did you know?

Kinshasa lies across the River Congo from Brazzaville, the capital of the Republic of the Congo. The two cities are the closest country capitals in the world.

Kinshasa is shown here at night.

This woman sweeps the street clean outside her shop in Kinshasa.

Lubumbashi is a big city in the south. It is in a part of the Congo that has many copper mines. Kisangani and Matadi are busy ports on the River Congo. Goods are shipped into and out of these ports.

Matadi is the Congo's main port. It is halfway between Kinshasa and the Atlantic Ocean.

Congolese homes

In the cities, most flats are made of cement blocks. In poor areas, people live in small houses made of mud bricks and sticks.

Some people in the Congo are refugees. They have left nearby countries that are at war. Refugees often live in tents in crowded camps.

People live in flats in this narrow building in Kinshasa. On the ground floor are shops.

In the country, most people live in houses of dried mud and sticks. The thatched roofs are made of grass or palm leaves. People who have more money might live in a house with a metal roof. They collect the rainwater that runs off it to use in the home. Poor people must collect water from a village pump or a river.

Women weave palm leaves to make a thatched roof.

This two-floor home is made of dried mud and has a thatched roof.

Food

Most people in the Congo eat just one or two meals a day. They eat a lot of starchy foods, such as corn, cassava and rice. Cassava or rice is cooked and then served in a big bowl. People reach in with one hand and help themselves. They mix the rice or cassava with a spicy sauce and shape the mixture into balls before eating it.

Women pound cassava roots (shown above) to make flour. The flour is used to make cassava bread, a daily food.

Congolese people grow and eat bananas. They also cook meat in 'packets' made from banana leaves.

Bananas and plantains are important foods. They are eaten raw, fried, steamed or mashed.

In the cities, restaurants serve spicy stews. They are made with vegetables and chicken or beef. Goat and catfish are on the menu, too.

Did you know?

Some people in the Congo do not have much money to buy meat. Sometimes they eat bats or grubs, the young of certain insects. Grubs contain a lot of protein.

At work

Some people in the Congo grow crops to sell. They tap rubber trees for latex, a milky white liquid that is used to make rubber. To collect the latex, workers make cuts in the trees. People also grow palm trees for oil. Farmers grow and sell cotton and coffee, too.

Did you know?
The latex collected from rubber trees is used in many ways including tyres, waterproof clothing and party balloons.

The latex trickles down the tree trunk and is collected in a bowl.

The Congo is very rich in natural resources. Much of the land in the Congo is covered with forests. People cut down trees for their wood, which is used to make furniture and in buildings.

A healthcare worker tests blood at a medical centre.

Villagers pan for diamonds in a river bed.

Mining is an important industry in the Congo. People mine diamonds, copper, gold and cobalt. Cobalt is a metal used to make jet engines and coloured glass.

In cities, people work in hotels, shops and banks. They teach in schools and work in health clinics and hospitals. Some people work in factories, making tyres, shoes, clothing and cement.

Having fun

Many people in the Congo like sport, especially football. They play on the streets and at school. They watch their favourite teams play at sports stadiums. Basketball and track and field are popular sports, too. People in the Congo and other parts of Africa like to play a board game called mancala.

A Congolese man returns the ball during a game of tennis in Kinshasa.

Football has many fans among the Congolese people. Here, the Democratic Republic of the Congo's national team plays a match against South Africa.

Did you know?

Traditional Congolese dances celebrate big events in life, such as the birth of a child or a good growing season for crops.

Music and dance are a big part of life in the Congo. People in villages play wooden flutes, beat on drums, dance and sing. In the cities, especially Kinshasa, many people enjoy dancing at nightclubs. Jazz music is popular, too.

Christmas and Easter are the main religious holidays. A special holiday is Parents' Day. On that day, 1st August, families go to cemeteries. They honour dead relatives by cleaning their graves. Later, the families have a picnic together.

The Congo: the facts

• The Democratic Republic of the Congo was renamed in 1997. Before then, the country was called Zaire.

• The Congo used to be ruled by Belgium. In 1960, the Congo gained independence from Belgium. People celebrate Independence Day on 30th June each year.

• In the past, the Congo has not been a true democracy. The people did not elect their leaders. Instead, one leader, a dictator, was the head of the country. Since 1990, the Congo's government has slowly given its people more freedom. Recently, the people voted for a president who is the head of the government.

The flag of the Democratic Republic of the Congo has a blue background. The colour blue stands for peace. A yellow star in the corner stands for the hope of a bright future.

Did you know?

The okapi is a symbol of the Congo. This animal does not live anywhere else in the world!

Okapis are related to giraffes. They have long tongues to grasp leaves – and also use them to clean their eyes and ears!

• The Congo is a country of unrest. At times, its people are at war with one another and with neighbouring countries.

The Congo's unit of money is the Congolese Franc.

Glossary

Ancestors family members who lived in the past.

Bonobo a type of great ape, similar to the chimpanzee.

Canopy the top layer of branches and leaves that covers a rainforest.

Cassava a starchy root vegetable.

Catfish a type of bony fish, which has an organ near the mouth similar to a cat's whiskers.

Continent a large land mass.

Copper a reddish-brown metal.

Democracy a government in which the people elect their leaders.

Dictator one leader who rules a country in which the people have no power.

Ethnic groups groups of people with the same cultures, traditions and ways of life.

Natural resources resources supplied by nature, such as coal and wood.

Palm a tropical tree with large leaves and no branches.

Plantains banana-like fruits that grow in tropical places.

Protein an important part of the food we eat. It is found in meat, dairy products and pulses such as beans.

Rainforest a very thick forest in a tropical climate where tall trees form a canopy.

Refugees people who flee their country, often for political or religious reasons.

Savannas areas of grasslands with few trees.

Starchy foods foods that contain starch, an important part of the food we eat. Starch is found in bread, potatoes and other foods.

Suburbs areas of housing that are outside the city centre.

Thatch a roof made of bundles of grass, palm leaves or straw.

Tropical very hot and damp.

Find out more

www.bbc.co.uk/nature/wildfacts
A wildlife A-Z by the BBC, with photographs and fact sheets about many animals including the okapi and bonobo.

www.nationalgeographic.com/congotrek360
Take a virtual tour of the River Congo area.

http:news.bbc.co.uk/cbbcnews/hi/guides/default.stm
Click on 'Africa' to learn about life on this vast continent.

Note to parents and teachers: Every effort has been made by the Publishers to ensure that these websites are suitable for children, that they are of the highest educational value, and that they contain no inappropriate or offensive material. However, because of the nature of the Internet, it is impossible to guarantee that the contents of these sites will not be altered. We strongly advise that Internet access is supervised by a responsible adult.

Congolese languages

Hundreds of languages are spoken in the Congo. French is the language of government because the Congo was once part of the Belgian Empire. Swahili, Lingala, Kikongo and Tshiluba are four of the main African languages used by Congolese people. You could try out some Swahili.

English	Swahili
hello	jambo
goodbye	kwaheri
how are you?	habari?
okay	sawa sawa
please	tafadhali
thank you	asante
no problem	hakuna matata
yes	ndiyo
no	hapana
I am hungry	nina njaa
food	chakula
water	maji

My map of the Congo

Trace this map, colour it in and use the map on page 5 to write the names of all the places.

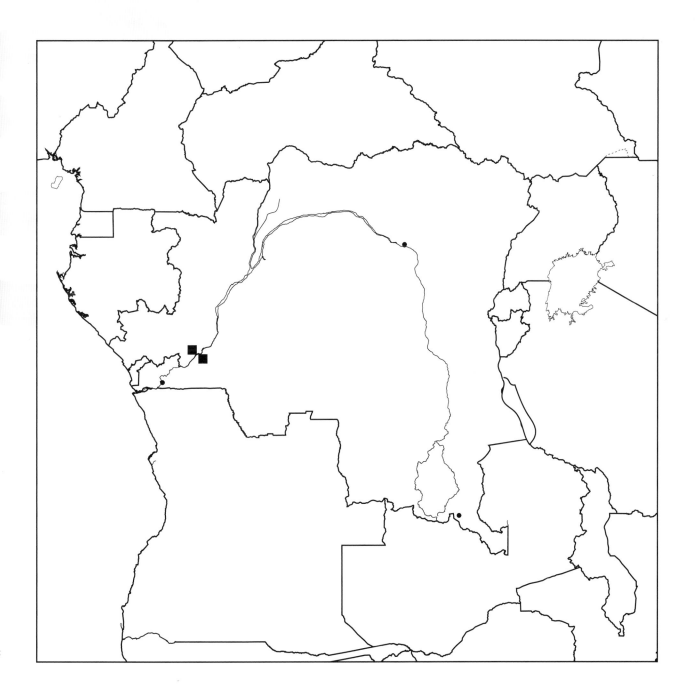

Index